Back of Beyond

Acknowledgements

Many of these poems appeared in Geoff Hattersley's previous publications:
The Deep End (Echo Room Press 1986)
Slouching Towards Rotherham (Wide Skirt Press 1987)
Shadows On The Beach (Red Sharks Press 1987)
The New Right (Smith/Doorstop Books 1987)
Port Of Entry (Littlewood Press 1989)
Split Shift (Smith/Doorstop Books 1990)
The Saxophonist's Eyes (Echo Room Press 1990)
The Good Stuff (Wide Skirt Press 1990)
Don't Worry (Bloodaxe Books 1994)
On The Buses With Dostoyevsky (Bloodaxe Books 1998)
Harmonica (Wrecking Ball Press 2003)

Some of the poems are included on a CD recorded with musician Michael Massey: *Death's Boots* (Wrecking Ball Records 2006).

Back of Beyond
New & Selected Poems

Geoff Hattersley

Smith/Doorstop Books

Published 2006 by
Smith/Doorstop Books
The Poetry Business
The Studio
Byram Arcade
Westgate
Huddersfield HD1 1ND

ISBN 1-902382-77-3

British Library Cataloguing-in-Publication Data. A
catalogue record for this book is available from the
British Library.

Typeset at The Poetry Business
Printed by H Charlesworth & Co, Wakefield

Cover picture: 'Irish Gothic', Jock McFadyen, 1987,
oill on canvas, 206x214 cm, Wolverhampton Art
Gallery

Distributed by Central Books Ltd., 99 Wallis Road,
London E9 5LN

The Poetry Business gratefully acknowledges the help
of Arts Council England and Kirklees Culture and
Leisure Services.

CONTENTS

For Jeanette

The Cigar

The cigar was huge. It was carried in
by three underfed slave-children in chains.

Everything stopped: spoons on their paths to mouths,
footsie under tables, all the soft words.

The President glanced round slowly
with the beginnings of an imbecilic grin…

Before the stunned gapes of the other customers,
he summoned a blow-torch and lit the thing.

It began to expand at an alarming rate,
taking a new, strange form, developing

what seemed to be a head. One woman abandoned
her life's jewellery, collapsed to the ground moaning

'Give it *me*! Give it *me*!' Her husband, tears streaming,
gobbled a photograph of their lovely children.

Waiters rushed to and fro with bowls of hot veal soup,
their bow-ties on the verge of hysteria.

Chandeliers fell crashing; in the darkness,
bottles of wine hopped back to the cellar,

remarkable creatures leapt from their plates,
forked just in time by the sweating manager.

The President celebrated
by loudly eating the whole five-pound lump

of garlic stilton with port wine on the dessert trolley.
The room was small and becoming increasingly

smaller. There seemed no escape

He Was Certainly An Intellectual

He'd be there, poised with red pen
over the latest collection of Steiner essays,

eager to underline
everything obvious to you or me.

He liked to talk about famous literary figures:
Lawrence, Hardy, Eliot, Conrad, James –

they were all such wonderful people
who'd done such wonderful things.

He could talk for hours and hours.
Hadn't he written twenty-two hundred

letters over the years to *The Observer*?
Hadn't he read *Heart of Darkness*

seventeen times?
He could assure you he had.

Christmas Shopping

You were writing dud cheques
like no one's business,
I was splashing
the forged tenners around.

In the hole in the road
someone sang
'Take Me to Tulsa',
snow settling on his sombrero.
I tossed him a tenner
screwed into a ball.

A woman approached
armed with documents
and truth;
she was selling badges,
a definite bargain
at a tenner apiece.

I signed the petition
to end the war.
I do a lot
of possibly useless writing.

That Weekend, You Wore

a tragic expression and were
loaded with meaningful glances.

We walked along the beach whipped
by sand on the wind, poked
at crabs half-eaten by gulls

and later, on the boating lake,
lost the oars and were forced
to abandon ship in the high wind.

There had to be a toilet
somewhere, but we couldn't find it,
so you disappeared into a bush,

and an old man's eyes grew wide
as he hobbled by – my clothes
dripping wet, a bent fag in my lips,

murmuring sweet nothings to a bush.

Because

Because his face did not fit
he walked in sideways, on his hands,
pushing a wheelbarrow loaded with groceries.

His moustache sweating, he pogo-danced the bump
toward the bowl of tulips, grabbed a bunch,
ate them noisily while whistling 'Little Stevie'.

He gave piggy-back rides to all the pregnant women.
He impersonated a trout on the end of a hook.
He applauded their insults

because his face did not fit.
And if it's true he didn't 'get the joke',
it's also true the joke wasn't very funny.

Readers

I have readers, they add up
to twenty, and I know at least
five women who're half-impressed.

Think of this: showing a book
by a friend to your mother,
your mother in the apron and slippers.
'He reminds me of you,' she says,
tossing the book aside, 'barmy.'

It can take years to get this far, years.

Shadows On The Beach

On the beach at Dahab, the sand was hot.
It felt good to sit there, to be naked
and take things easy, to glance out to where
the women plunged shouting into the sea.
On the radio, Jim Morrison wanted
to be loved two times, Ba-by, loved twice today.

A small Bedouin girl aproached,
a shadow on the pages of my book.
I looked up, smiled. Shyly, she asked
if she could eat the apple-core
I'd just dropped in the sand.

Diary Of A Week In September

Don't ask me how
but Sunday never happened.

Monday, I blinked for an instant,
it was suddenly Tuesday.

That's when I fell asleep
while planning for Wednesday.

I woke on Thursday, spent the day
wondering where was Wednesday?

Friday you said was really
Thursday, and before we knew

where we were it was Saturday.
Some things needed dusting

and there was a shopping list
as long as *The Log of the Sloop Exceed*.

The Man At Number Ten

slams his front door:

there goes a man who
takes himself seriously,

shoulders hunched
for passers-by,

always busy
going nowhere, fast.

He spends every Sunday
with his head in an engine,

every single evening
throwing darts at a board.

He seems content
with a dog and a wife,

I've sometimes seen him
take one or both for a walk.

Theology

A good friend of mine
one day; the next,
someone who just happened
to look like her.

'God tapped me on the shoulder,'
she said
and handed me the leaflet.

Returning home on the bus
I heard one schoolgirl
telling another
'Simon Bletsoe put his hand
on my fanny last night.'

Later, the same one
tapped me on the shoulder
to ask for a light.

Almost Unbelievably

Sad, to be sitting here still
smoking too many cigarettes,
watching this cold pancake of a film
for the third time in one life,

to consider my mother,
patiently sitting through Western
after Western with my father
because she *liked the scenery*.

History repeats itself, after
a fashion, and these also
are facts: the diaries we've kept
aren't worth the paper they're scrawled on,

our stamp collection –
let's face it, it's dull.
When the toast caught fire
last night and the grill,

it was the most exciting event
here for at least three years.

Desert

We were out in the desert, just sort of
fooling around, dreaming up names for some
loud, long-haired rock band we'd be sure to form
the minute we got back home. I liked most

Doctor Straight Neck and his Toothpick Killers.
That was when Heidi started laughing and
couldn't stop – as much the drink and heat as
the wit, I guess. But it was good, hearing

her laugh like that, after all she'd been through.
The desert could do that. Such stillness there,
as if the earth was taking breath, as if
history was yet to be invented.

I look after cacti in the house now.
They don't take much of that. I never did
keep in touch with any of those people,
though I heard Heidi died in Berlin, smack.

Love Poem

Alan hates John and Pete.
Pete hates Alan and John.
John hates Pete but not Alan.
I hate Pete and Alan

and John. Alan hates me.
Pete and John might hate me
for all I know. Nev hates
no one. No one hates Nev, though

the two boys from Dover
hate the lot of us. We hate
the two boys from Dover.
The two girls from Finchley

hate John and would hate Alan
too if they knew he read
their diaries. We all hate
the people we see with

money, the people who buy
groceries. The people
hate us also. I hate
the smell of France and its wine.

Days

Our lives in yawning
back-to-backs,
mud and dogshit dragged
across acres of carpet,
so many kettles
boiling and boiled.

It has come to this,
that when we step round
the puddle the rushing car
will spray us head to foot,
that when we smile
at the neighbour she'll say
*Who the fuck do you think
you're laughing at?*

These are the days
to sit with music:
Jaco Pastorius
re-defining electric bass
as easily as most people
breathe.

Toast

I worry too much
about the past, silly things:

leaving my mother's
plastic breadbin
on the grill-top
while making toast,

the men who said they'd
kill me before long.

Then there was Israel:
spent cartridges
and blood by the roadside,

and the noise, everywhere.

How She Puts It

'It's about time you grew up,' she says,
as though he doesn't know that theory.

'All I said,' he starts to say
but she's not interested

in all he said, slamming
the door as she leaves.

He's both feet on her coffee table
when she later tells him it's over:

'Get out and take your ugliness with you,'
is how she puts it.

Briefcase

Life makes as much sense to me
as a ripe avocado does to a dog.
I was passed an unsigned cheque
by a man impersonating a friend

and got back home to a cold meal.
I found a man's black leather briefcase
in the corner of the bedroom
and knew it was my own.

Threatening At Any Moment To Blush

The girl is telling me she doesn't like
poetry, not really, not much, only
Brian Patten, John Cooper-Clarke and Joolz

and now me. This is new and exciting,
to be signing books for girls just left school
unsure yet how to hold a cigarette

and a half-lager in the same small hand.
I finish with a flourish, and then X,
and the girl stays a while, smiling a lot,

blushing a lot, glimpses of a party
I reckon I'd be happy to gatecrash.
But I stay sober in the face of it,

as though someone had tapped on my shoulder
to whisper, 'Hey, you're a married man, now.'
Which is what happened, more or less.

Meatballs, Jerusalem, Tattoo

The beer was warm but I drank it all the same,
and ate the meatballs, two on a white plate, a little gravy,

while the proprietor offered various photographs of himself,
his sexual acts with European women,

proudly, like showing off family snapshots to a tired colleague,
the meatballs going down slowly, needing to be chewed well.

I saw the tattooed number on the old woman's arm
as I studied Hamsun and Pound in the bookshop.

The Drummer

He claimed to be a drummer
just a drummer

though we couldn't help but notice
the sticks in his hands, the obscenity

the way he'd stare, stare
ahead as he drummed

disturbing with his drums
his *drumming* the neighbourhood

stirring things up, things
best left unstirred, yes

at times *directly polemical*
this this this this drummer.

We could break his hands
and we did break them.

Spider

The spider was completely unprepared
for assault from above by an ashtray.

It never had a friend it could count on.
It never knew its blood group.

It never saw itself changing, or any need to.
It never said: 'No more excuses.'

It never felt tempted by drugs.
It never knew the itch to the nearest bar.

Its earning power was never an issue.
It was never hurt by a few home truths.

It never did anything for anyone.
It never knew the myth of Wyatt Earp.

It never hoped for more than was likely.
It never had Watchtower thrust at it.

It never saw a rainbow, or a bunch of flowers
dropped into an open grave.

It never wrote an essay on the works of Alexander Pope.
It never filled in an application form.

It never married for love or money.
It never had a honeymoon in a hotel.

It never knew who was Prime Minister.
It never knew if it was lucky or not.

It never shopped for clothes.
It never smiled.

It never felt like a paperclip
in a jar in a cupboard in a shed.

It never carried a briefcase.
It never missed the last train.

It never slept off a hangover.
It never thought it was Marlon Brando.

It never grew a beard, or shaved in cold water.
It never fished in the Mississippi.

It never heard rumours about itself.
It never had to face its inadequacy.

It never had any wild ideas.
It never had any wild ideas drummed out of it.

It never laughed at a copper's helmet.
It never gave a false name and address.

It never saw the Marx Brothers, or listened to Sgt. Pepper.
It never knew what was in fashion.

It never got careless, or said it was past caring.
It never left its clothes lying in a heap.

It never preferred to remain anonymous.
It never wondered who wrote Shakespeare

or invented light-bulbs.
It never thought it would win an award one day.

It never moved because it didn't like the neighbourhood.
It never fastened its seat-belt for a rough ride.

It never played a guitar that had just one string.
It never looked for warts in its armpits.

It never turned its back on the dreams of its youth.
It never felt guilty for wasting time.

It never considered circumcision.
It never got hard-ons travelling by bus.

It never got sentimental at Christmas.
It never thought the carpet and curtains clashed.

It never spent a night awake with its partner
wishing the photograph album empty.

It never read about itself on the front page.
It never had more than its fair share of problems.

It was never diagnosed manic-depressive.
It was never found guilty of a thing.

It never made a list of things to do.
It never waited for the right partner to come along,

or became half of a couple with a headache between them.
It never dropped earwax in the ashtray.

It never had a first at the races.
It never tied a donkey to someone sleeping.

It never had a pension plan.
It never wanted to impress itself,

or thought it was better than it was.
It never got serious over the funniest things.

It never had a boss for a friend,
or a friend who thought he was a boss.

It never stared out to sea, it never watched the tide come in.
It never worried whether or not it created a good impression.

It never took notice of a roadsign.
It never put a barbed-wire fence up.

It never wept inside headphones, briefly.
It never learned to think things over more,

to peep before it plunged.
It never took its shoes off to save the carpet.

It never learned to spell archaeologist.
It never scratched its arse in a food queue.

It never read a book about Hitler.
It never met a neo-oligarch.

It never used washing powder, or learned to start a fire.
It never used a telephone box.

It never accepted a cigarette.
It never laughed at its own joke.

It never sat in the back row,
or dreamt it was the steering wheel through James Dean's chest.

It never grew its hair to its shoulders.
It never picked its feet on the bed.

It never had a twenty-first birthday party.
It never washed its hands of anybody.

It never needed an explanation, or a diet.
It never said: 'Too gentle for my liking, too jolly.'

It never taught itself German, telling its partner
to be quiet so it could concentrate.

It never worried about what it was swallowing.
It never looked for heroes and villains.

It never smiled apologetically.
It never pressed a blade into its wrist.

It never wished it lived in a caravan.
It never fried bacon and eggs.

It never felt like a fat catalogue
of books published in limited editions

no one wants anyhow, not at any price.
It never tore a book in half.

It never felt like it was an abstract
that has everybody shaking their heads.

It never had a gun held to its head.
It never felt a wire tightened round its throat.

It was completely unprepared
for assault from above by an ashtray.

Problems With The Overflow

You don't like to lose your cool and you don't
often. If you do, you think of a machine
that moves through the streets chopping legs off at the knees
and now the kids on the corner whistle
the funeral procession as you pass them.
But you're pretty thick-skinned and can take it
and there's always something to keep you from brooding:
a door that won't open or a door that won't close,
an overflow that keeps overflowing
or signs of strength or weakness in a rival.
What do you care if someone else freezes
in a bath they should have emptied?
You listened through the wall as he sang: he was deep
as a country 'n' western compilation
and with the same belief in the double-negative,
crackling like a 78 when he should have been a CD.
If his future was a building it would be demolished
but it's nothing to you since you woke up
and lit a fire – not a large one, about
the size of a copper's helmet or head.

Not far from where you spit, a family play
croquet on the lawn. There's a bright steel skateboard
poking under their gate like a machine.

Slaughterhouse

At last, I was ready to say goodbye
to a tether made of fishnet stockings.
My friends told me not to, that I needed
a bandage for my head, needed a crutch for it.
I muttered Jolly Good like a jolly fellow,
caught the next bus. When I got where it was going
a man tried to sell me a Coke for five dollars.
I asked the next for the way to the slaughterhouse.
He told me to follow the smell of blood and bone.
The smell was powerful, at some distance even.

*

The first time I ate grilled octopus tentacles –
a strange moment, one I feel a need to mention.
An undercover cop had leeched onto me at a bar,
between mouthfuls of ouzo and tentacles
was pretending to be the greatest punk rock band ever.
He asked if I wanted to dance, the meathook
in my hand was reassuring. He loved every minute
of his pathetic life. Young men with sticks
surrounded our piled-high table
after he told the barman he should fuck his bill.

*

The morning after I ate grilled octopus tentacles
a man helped me buy powder in the pharmacy,
took me by the arm and found me a hotel room.
I was embarrassed among strangers the rest of the day –
they were passing round photos taken on the beach
that summer I weighed fifteen and a half stone.
At night I searched every room in the place,
sifting through bins stuffed with used tampons and shit-roll
for one small thing that would let me know where I was.
The landlady joined me about half-two.

*

I did press-ups and pull-ups and ran on the spot.
I brushed my teeth and shaved away three months
of enthusiastic cunnilingus.
I practised speaking without using shit and fuck
and held myself erect. Bumping into her on the stairs
I complimented her on her repertoire
but suggested she make more of a noise.
What do I most wish now, as I pick my teeth here
some years later? That she had understood a word I said
and that my nose hadn't been so obviously running.

*

The slaughterhouse started my head pounding
and there is a harsh sound, a hundred cows
screaming in unison. I went nuts there
and then. Years of treatment would have followed
if I hadn't escaped the building that minute.
I hitched a lift with a man who told me
I had good legs, sexy legs. He needed glasses
and a room at a hotel, I replied –
did he have his wallet? Yes he did. His head cracked
as he landed in the road, I didn't look back.

*

What I fell in love with was her singing,
not that it was what you'd call good singing.
It would reach me in my room as I lay naked
in the baked afternoons, talking aloud
to the insects on the ceiling and walls.
It was the happiness that surprised me,
and how it lingered a long time after.
I was never a music critic, no,
Not bad, I'd say, turning this way and that,
looking in the mirror at my pale face.

Trouble

He makes no more noise than a cactus plant.
He's closed the curtains and left the lights off.

He knows his enemies won't let it drop.
They'll stick his head on a pole, dance round it.

He's closed the curtains and left the lights off.
He thinks of a room with a door with no handle.

*

They'll stick his head on a pole, dance round it.
He should have listened to what friends told him.

He thinks of a room with a door with no handle.
He'd like that room. He'd like that door a lot.

He should have listened to what friends told him:
You go there with that face you can expect trouble.

*

He'd like that room, he'd like that door. A lot.
The thing he just can't get out of his head's

You go there with that face you can expect trouble.
Nothing's a joke, nothing's funny, nothing.

The thing he just can't get out of his head's
he knows his enemies won't let it drop.

Nothing's a joke, nothing's funny, nothing.
He makes no more noise than a cactus plant.

Minus Three Point Six

Suppose there are three doors:
Religion, Insanity, Suicide.
Suppose you're on TV,
the hostess asks which door you'll take.
Suppose ten million viewers

and a studio audience of enemies
are all shouting their preference
and in the din the hostess mishears:
you ask for Religion, get Insanity.
You're shoved through and the door closes.

You try to shout for help, you want
to explain there's been a mistake,
you can't, can't move, feel as if
you're held in place by chains
or a pair of huge hands.

It's so dark you can't see yourself,
so quiet you could hear a plant move
though there are none moving.
There are no words in your head, just numbers.
You try but can't stop thinking about them.

One and one is two plus seventeen is eighteen
minus three point six is fifteen point eight
multiplied by twenty-seven point seven is
four thousand three hundred and sixty-five point six
divided by five point five is

Hannon In A Nutshell

His gripe was with the whole world, everybody,
and it seemed no amount of money
would put a smile on that long face.
His seventh album, called *Seventh Album*,
bristled with unresolved grievances,
'The Big Ships' and 'On The Other Hand'
the tracks that attracted most attention.
In the former, a solitary piano chord
repeated at five-second intervals
as Hannon grunted his ex-wife's name
was the sparest rock recording
since the heyday of Haddock Potion.
'On The Other Hand', on the other hand,
was its antithesis, a wild incantation
positively celebrating his loneliness,
the twenty-five percussionists
taking it into uncharted territory.
It is a stunning, twisted performance,
shocking as an amputation, perhaps
completely paranoid.

Hannon's mental decline over the following years
is well-documented elsewhere. Suffice to say
the Nixon Holiday Inn disturbance
was not an isolated incident
and the artistic output suffered correspondingly.
His relevance to the young of today
can be summed up thus: there but for the grace of God
could have gone your dad.

Don't Worry

A man in the Elephant and Castle
said there were games I should know more about,
I should try fags on the backs of my hands
or taking a shotgun to bed with me.
I recalled him dropped in the street one night,
the fine crack in his skull, the blood, the cold,
the copper who didn't think he'd make it.
'I tell thee lad, listen, what I don't know
about masturbation's not worth knowing.'
The place was suddenly brighter, I realised
he couldn't see me, he wasn't talking
to me at all. His brother came in then
with the news Clothes Line wouldn't be coming,
they'd been in a pile-up, all their gear
was written off. A girl who followed them
from gig to gig began to shake her head.
'Don't worry,' I told her, 'no one was hurt
except the bass player. His ribs showed through
his blood-soaked shirt as they tried to free him
from the snare drum.' I drank up and set off
along the canal, kicking at loose stones,
whistling one of the old songs I'm sick of,
sometimes stopping to see if I could spit
hard enough to reach the opposite bank.

.

Nobel Prize Poem

He awoke with no hangover
because he'd had no beer
and looked in the mirror.
He couldn't help noticing
that a box of old records
not worth listening to
teetered on his neck
in place of a head.
He tied his shoelaces.
He was barefoot.

*

At the time, he was seeing
a Scandanavian woman
whose life was her watercolours:
orange skies, pink highways.
She wanted to live in a cave
and win the Nobel Prize.
I'm not interested
in saving the world, he told her,
it's hard enough remembering
to change my underpants.

*

Then he wrote a story
about a bad writer
and thirty-seven people
sent him insulting letters:
How dare he portray them
in such a callous manner?
He couldn't even remember
meeting fourteen of them.
Three or four of them
were actually good writers.

Eccentric Hair

There was something grinning on the telly:
Everything's creative, it said, meaning
staring at a shadow on the ceiling.
I didn't switch off, just sort of grunted.
I wasn't good for much at the time
except worrying about the first post
coming ten minutes after the second,
the cop who parked outside my house reading
How The CIA Murdered Bob Marley
and the gangsters who tailed me when I went
to the bank, to the shops, to the dentist.
I was low, listening to the same song
over and over: *Don't Tell Me You Don't Believe It*
                    & Call Yourself A Friend
and I'd no idea what I wanted,
other than to be able to relax
and see the funny side of things again,
maybe think back to being seventeen,
wishing I was Bob Dylan or someone
or at least had pretty eccentric hair.
I just needed to get out more, out of the house.

My suit was at the drycleaners so I wore jeans
and a denim jacket. I leaned against the bar
avoiding the eyes of the other customers:
the place was full of all the fools I'd ever been.
I heard them getting more and more maudlin.

Hyphen

The party was like the hyphen in Seymour-Smith.
The men were a stiff bunch, the women even worse.
I ended up pretending I'd the shits:
'Must have been the meat, I'm not used to it.'
We needed great mouthfuls of air, walked rather than
take a taxi. Jeanette took her shoes off
and her feet got dirty. She washed them in the sink
while I picked up a book. I read aloud,
it was pretty funny. You know the book I mean.
There was a lot of noise outside: dogs, screams,
and Jeanette came and peered through the curtains,
leaving a trail of damp, talcumed footprints
which I pointed out when she turned back round.
'When are you going to get your clothes off?' she said.

Elsecar Reservoir

Although languid on the surface
Elsecar reservoir is dangerous
to swim in. Underwater currents
can grab and drag you down
into a system of potholes.

I hear myself say this
and can hardly believe it.
Jeanette turns away, startled.
Old people are feeding ducks,
a few fishermen sit still.

Pike are another reason
for not swimming, I say.
They've been known to swallow
whole men, boys anyway,
let's put it like this –

It's looking like rain
says an old man with a cap
and a dog that cowers.
It weren't forecast though
he adds as he passes.

Let's put it like this,
you definitely wouldn't want
to go swimming with the fuckers.
I stop and sit on the bank,
feeling in my pocket for my fags.

One of the fishermen pulls in
a strange object, nothing
like a fish. Everyone

stands around discussing it
as it flip-flops on the bank

then suddenly it's down the bank and gone
before anyone can stop it.
Two girls aged four and six
start to cry in the next street.
We can hear them clearly

till the brass band starts up.
That's funny, Jeanette says,
I can hear a brass band
but I can't see it.
Seventy-Six Trombones is what they play.

In Phil's Butchers

They're sure they know me from somewhere:
'Aren't tha t' bloke that rode naked
on a bike through Jump for charity?
Thi picture wa' in t' Chronicle.'
The previous customer leaves, coughing
something red and green onto the pavement.
'That's a poorly mister, dead on 'is feet 'e is.'
One of them decides he worked
with my brother at Johnson's
though I've no brother who worked there.
'Are tha sure?' he wonders.
An older man (is it Phil?)
pops his head in from the back room:
'Leave t' lad alone 'n' gi' 'im 'is pies.'
I hold them in my hand as I say 'Ta-ra'
and leave, taking off my dark glasses.
There's a patch of blue sky
where my eyes should be, which startles
an old woman crossing the road.
'By,' I say, to reassure her,
'it's cold enough for a walking stick.'
'All laughter is despair,' she replies,
'it's t' human condition, like.'

Remembering Dennis's Eyes

He always blinked too much,
like an overnight guest who leaves
with the toilet paper in his holdall
or leaves a dry blanket
covering a wet bed.
Even with the balaclava
turned round to hide his face
I could see him blinking
through the makeshift eyeholes.

Gimme the bastard bag
he yelled, tugging at it.
The iron bar bounced on
the guard's helmet five times
before he fell to his knees,
another four or five before
he lost his grip on the bag.
Tha saw nowt, nowt, Dennis hissed,
pinning me to the wall
with one hand, waving the bar
like a conductor with the other.

The last time I saw him,
years later, years ago,
he'd just tried to strangle his ex-wife,
had been stopped by
his ten-year-old daughter.
He was running toward Darfield
like a wind-up toy
with a pair of kitchen scissors
sticking between his shoulder-blades.

Death's Boots

for Ian McMillan

In a previous incarnation, I climbed mountains
and sang my own praises, anticipating the trend.

On each wall of my home hung gaudy self-portraits.
I was posing for the camera before I invented it.

Then I was told I was a fool, that my career was over
for perfecting the ever-lasting light-bulb.

So I took a post kicking the oats out of farmers.
The money was good. Death's Boots, they called me.

I became involved because I saw no reason not to.
The reasons would pile up later like wood-shavings

from the pencils of the man who wrote *The American Century*.
That man was me, Death's Boots.

The Only Son At The Fish 'n' Chip Shop

He lived with his mother till he was forty-five
and no one was allowed to touch his head.

He worked on a novel for twenty years
without writing a word. He didn't like people

who wrote novels. He often drank. One glass of beer
was too many, two glasses weren't enough.

Travel brochures were as far as he went.
A football match, one time. He often said

'Why would anyone want to think about a potato?'
He painted his door with nobody's help.

The Persuaders

A well-known nobody
is opening The Countryman in Wombwell
and some people are ridiculous enough
to turn up and ask for his autograph.
He's ridiculous enough to sign them.
Twenty years on, we sit arguing

over who it was: Tony Curtis? Or
Roger Moore, before he was James Bond?
The beer's warm and a rockabilly band
are trying to pretend electricity
hasn't been invented. The harmonies are great
if you like that kind of thing. When we leave

the six of us walk in single file
up the narrow street that takes us
past The Angler's Rest and The Ship
and the Conservative and Catholic clubs
and British Legion and Royal Oak
and The Alma and Little George
and into the Horse Shoe,
where the barmaid is a comedienne:
'Good evening, ladies and beasts.'
It's Nev's round.

On the Buses with Dostoyevsky

Because of the steelworks
that deafened my dad
our telly was always
too loud, so loud
it formed a second narrative
to what I was reading
up in my room
in my late teens – I'd have
Hemingway and *Kojak*,
Alias Smith and Jones and Poe.
All that noise! Car chases
and gunshots, sirens, screams,
horse racing and boxing,
adverts for fishfingers,
floor cleaner and fresh breath;
and Knut Hamsun starving,
Ahab chasing his whale.
I felt like a learner driver
stalled at a traffic light,
a line of lorries behind me.
Because of the steelworks
that closed in 1970
I like silence and calm,
I like silence and smoke
cigarettes in the dark.

Grace

died in a hospital bed
surrounded by her family.
She'd been unconscious
days on end
then suddenly sat up and
looked her husband
right in the eye.
They were both
eighty-three.

I sat there
a while, just her and me.
I wanted to believe
somehow, somewhere, something
of her still lived.
I held her hand,
recalled a dream I'd had
when I was four.
Grace saved me from a lion,
beating it off with a poker
at the top of the cellar steps.

Holy Air

I

This is where Jesus died and was reborn.
It's illegal to drive a bus unarmed
and the drivers wear side-holsters,
strut round the station like a posse.
A dozen soldiers share the seats with you,
nursing their rifles, never letting go.

This is where Jesus was resurrected
and the bazaars are full of it.
You need money, a lot,
and Arabs will follow you down the street –
'I can sell you a jar of Holy Air
at a reasonable price.'

II

'This street is closed,'
says a young Arab boy
suddenly blocking my path,
'bad muslims.'
He holds out his hand
and I give him a shequel
as the call to prayer
rolls across the rooftops.
God is great! he shouted
as he detonated the bomb
strapped to his chest.
Something like this happens
and does not stop.

Not For Aesthetic

I'm to work with Mario,
an Argentinian carpenter
who's been on the kibbutz
six years. He arrives
on a bicycle, a white Labrador
trailing behind. With winter
peeping round the corner,
it's important we paint
the outside of some new
wooden buildings. 'Not
for aesthetic, but to…'
He blinks behind his glasses
and waves his hands.
'Protect,' I say.
'Yes,' he says.
Today though the sun is hot
and I take off my shirt,
can feel my back roasting
as I slap grey paint.
It's hard to believe
it's November; back home
they'll be buttoning big coats,
wrapping their scarves.
But Mario insists
that here too it will be cold
and raining before long.
He constantly apologises
for his English:
'I study it five years
two hours each week
but I never speak it.'
Really I have no trouble
understanding him, though
he doesn't seem to get

much of what *I* say.
'It's my northern accent,'
I tell him, 'we're poor
and can't speak properly.'
'In Argentina, the south
poor and the north…'
'Prosperous.'
'Yes.' And later,
the work done, walking home,
Mario pushing his bicycle
and the dog trotting
alongside, nosing the grass
for lizards or hedgehogs,
I try to tell him more
about the north of England –
the pits shut, the unemployment,
Thatcher's legacy.
'In my country,' he says,
'we call the Malvinas
Thatcher's war.'
The dog runs barking
to the foot of a tree.
'In mine too,' I reply
in my clearest English.
He nods, and shouts something
at the now frantic dog.

November

The young Israelis
accept their lot.
Here at this kibbutz breakfast table
are a dozen, boys and girls
who'll soon be soldiers.
And the long hair of the boys,
hanging over the backs
of their Jim Morrison
and Nirvana t-shirts,
or tied in ponytails,
and the rings through the noses
of the girls and some boys,
will go, must go, in March.
November, they sit
cheerfully eating eggs
and reading their newspapers
back to front, left to right:
five soldiers wounded slightly
near the Lebanese border;
one killed in a drive-by shooting
in the quiet town of Safad;
three killed, one left paralysed
by a suicide bomber
at Netzarim junction.
This is the daily news.
And I sit with them
and chew toast and jam,
thirty-eight and British
and safe, and wonder if
any will make the news
themselves.

Piper

At the age of thirty-seven
he owns only what he stands in
and enough stuff to fill a duffel bag
but he's not worried.
He stopped worrying about the future
the day he left Germany
to avoid the draft,
losing himself in Amsterdam
with a woman who could keep up.
He made a living.
The day the police arrested him
he had a ticket to see Dylan –
for more than one decade
this had been an ambition.
Instead, he got to spend two years
reading Albert Camus and Herman Hesse,
Charles Bukowski and Jack Kerouac.
It was like being back
in the orphanage.

Pale and skinny, hardly
a word to say for himself.
We see him quickly change
into a muscular, tanned raconteur,
holding court on his porch
all afternoon and evening
until something, the past
or some version of the future,
puts a bottle of vodka
firmly in his hand,
clouds his eyes.
And he's turning up for work drunk,
seven in the morning.

Something From a Stupor

He held a bottle of Gold Star up,
peered into it solemnly.
Told me for the tenth time
he was just 'one of the guys',
something reptilian
about the stare he fixed me with
through the green glass of the bottle.
He was young enough to be a son
I'd disown,
the sort of man who'd rip
somebody's photo to pieces.
He glanced from face
to face, grinning;
the two fat blokes at our table
left with their expensive cameras.
'We don't need them,' he said, and
laughed, 'I don't need anybody.'
Then the noise started, the disco,
and he was off and dancing,
leaving behind his untouched beer
and a smell like gunpowder.
I saw him only one more time, a glimpse,
just before the place closed
at five in the morning,
of a small group of men his own age
herding him through the door,
his cries
drowned out
by 'Trenchtown Rock'.

They Were Both Liars

Boring as well, though the girl
falling out of the window
story was at least
energetic. The eldest
was drunk, an idiot half the time,
unconscious the rest.
'You don't like to talk to me,' he said,
vodka in my face in a bus
on the way to the Dead Sea.
'No, I like to,' I replied,
'but not at six in the morning.'
That evening I'd see him
throw a mattress round a garden
furiously, shouting
in his own language.
I'd stand and watch
for a quarter of an hour.

The young one was different,
always talking about a phone call
he was expecting.
He pummelled a punchbag
suspended from a tree
for one hour each afternoon
beneath a scorching sun.
And he'd run, for one hour,
then sit staring into space
while he got his breath back
for two hours.
The day they escorted the drunk one
onto the bus, making it clear
he'd better not come back,
the punchbag one forgot
to punch his bag.
Then remembered.

The Chickens

Like a spiv
from the Second World War
he passes the chickens
through the dishwasher hatch,
turns and gets away quick
as I stuff them
in my laundry bag.

Two more hours
and the shift will be done.
I'll be in the shower,
then playing backgammon
in the afternoon sun.
The chickens defrosting.
None of us

can stomach
another kibbutz dinner –
cottage cheese, green peppers,
boiled eggs, stale bread.
The chickens down to me,
I'll sit back while the rest
do the work.

Tapping my feet
to the rhythm guitar.
The fire in the darkness,
our shapes huddled round it.
The meat sizzling, spitting.
The dogs inching closer,
told to lie down.

Bruise

Since I slipped
and spent fifteen minutes
on my back moaning
at the hub of a circle
of concerned and amused faces
I've had pins and needles
in my right hand. I thought
I'd broken my elbow
but it was only bruised.
The doctor gave me some painkillers
which have a real buzz,
better than the vodka – 'wodka'
it says on the bottles here.
Actually, the wodka
tastes like petrol, not that

I've ever drunk petrol.
Listen, a few minutes ago
I put down Norman's book.
It was archetypal Norman,
I mean he was just
blowing his own trumpet,
and he doesn't even have
a very good one –
he must have bought it
at Woolworth's
back in the seventies.
'What was the book like?' Jeanette asks.
'It was interesting,' I reply,
'as was having a toe amputated
when I was nineteen.'

The Barking of Stray Dogs

The barking of stray dogs
outside my window
in the middle of the night
doesn't bother me
any more, not a bit,
well maybe a bit.
So much is funny
it's hard to know where to finish –
behaving like one
of the Blues Brothers,
or spending the whole day
slicing carrots, a man of my
whatever.

Tequila is good
mixed with grapefruit,
if you've the patience
to squeeze them. Traffic passes
and is not noticed,
like the early stages
of a mental illness.
The locals' word for a hangover
is also their word
for a stray dog.

Politics

It's like watching a film
of your own funeral.
You're shouting I'M ALIVE
but no one can hear you.

Across a room, two men
assess each other's silence.
They yawn and cough,
cross and uncross thin legs.

It takes years.
Ice forms on the cameras
that bring us news.
And then the men nod,

and then they rise.
One claps, then holds up a hoop
the other leaps through.
They both shout BOOM!

Jupiter

I've been lost in a study of Jupiter.
Thirty-three hundred times the size of earth

but no movie industry to speak of,
hence no awards ceremonies and no

microphones in the faces of nothing.
I explained all this in the town centre

but people seemed eager to ignore me.
Ah, people. They like to think they know me

by my black moustache and curly red wig
and the wheelchair I push in front of me

containing the rag doll, ukulele,
and the ghetto blaster I sing along with.

They know my favourite song is 'Love Me Do',
which I croon to a punk backing, they know

my coat for all weathers is grey cotton.
They don't know how I ache in these old bones.

They know yobbos sometimes gang up on me.
They don't know what the boots taste like.

Rum and Blue Sky

It was the time of day he liked the most,
before everyone got busy.
Just the one drink, straight down, then he was out,
striding along the disused railway track,
his old dog barely able to keep up.
All those people! He had no time for them,
them or their dull regulations.
He'd had no choice in jail, they'd seen to that;
that was part of it. Well he was free now.
He reached the bridge where he always turned back;
the sky was a clear blue pressed handkerchief.
He felt the weight of the bottle, kissed it,
took a mouthful of rum and kept going.

Through it all he stayed true to his own dreams.
And here he was, breathing. Even his dog
seemed to hear the promise the day whispered
to soar like a frisbee thrown at the sun.
He was humming something joyful, something
he couldn't put a name to but knew well.

I Was an Unarmed Teenager

Sunday morning, just after nine
or just before, and the Salvation Army band
strike up a dirge
right under the window.
I roll my hangover
from one red eye to the other, sit up
and stare down at the musicians
in their uniforms, rasping
their dirty hankie tune –
I shoot them
through their mouthpieces
with an imaginary gun.

My mother's getting warm
in front of an open oven,
a pot of tea just made,
Sunday People on the table
open at the crossword page,
and the dog slobbers toward me
with prisoner's eyes
but he's no chance
of a walk on the canal bank
right now. 'How do you die
like a cowboy,' my mother asks,
'four-three-four?'

Cold Spot

I've taken to wearing
a jacket in the house,
it's colder than outside,
the walls are damp,
dripping sometimes,
this is a dump alright,
where I live, fastened in
with the noise of cars
and lorries streaming past,
in my head like harsh voices
or bad music, my breath
steaming up the window
as I stand watching
people without cars,
old, slow, cold, hanging on,
keeping death away
with whatever it takes
and their shopping bags.

I flush the toilet,
hear next door's baby
start to cry. I stand
and listen. It cries and
cries and cries.

Smoke

The first time I lit up in front of him
it was about midnight,
I was watching The Marx Brothers with Dave.
I was fifteen, Dave was thirteen,
my dad must have been thirty-eight.
I was gagging for a No. 6,
willing my dad to fall asleep
in the chair like he often did.
I think the film was *Room Service*;
something they weren't at their best in.
I stared. I got more and more tense.
In the end I just lit a fag
like it was the most natural thing
in the world for me to do
and my dad
stood very slowly,
walked out and up the stairs
without a word
for months.

Two Love Poems

(i) Younger, Fresher

I got my hair cut
this morning, too short
is how it looks to me
but she likes it, Jeanette.
She says it makes me look
younger, fresher.
She says it makes me look
as if I know I'm living a life
that could be
much worse.
'Do you like them?' she asks,
turning her feet this way and that
in some new black
high-heeled sandals.

(ii) Bed Poem

She holds me from behind
or I curl up to her,
I like to feel her warm
backside. Like a workman's
brazier, I tell her.
Go to sleep, she murmurs.

I'm sure someone once said
a poem should be like an
onion, peeling it, layer after layer
bringing tears to the eyes,
but who'd want to wake up
in bed with that person?

Splinter

i.m. Mona Eileen Hattersley, 1935-1998

She said it was too small for her to see
and too small for my dad to see
but she had a splinter in her finger,

it was driving her up the wall –
this was when she was about fifty-five
so I was about thirty-four.

She passed me a pair of tweezers,
told me to take the splinter out
if I could see it. I could see it alright

and I got it with the tweezers
and pulled it straight out, no messing,
and my mother gave a sigh of relief.

Eight years later she was full of cancer,
drugged up, surrounded by cards and flowers,
fussed over by strangers in uniforms.

We took her home for the last month, she insisted.
'They can't make a proper cup of tea here,' she said,
'it's no wonder everybody's badly.'

At This Table

I stare at the letter. It's from a young poet
who wants advice on how to get gigs in New York,
as if I could help him, barefoot and hungover

at this table in Huddersfield, up to my neck in shit.
This was meant to be my way out.
I'm laughing my head off the more I think of it.

I've been staying out of the sun, I get cold sores.
You have to avoid intimate oral contact,
where's the fun in that... Now Jeanette's telling me

about all the shopping trolleys in the canal
and on the bottom, plastic traffic cones.
The ducks appear unruffled however.

A Terrible Song

was just starting. I switched it off
and went to buy a loaf. I had the usual
small worries, sleeplessness
and being at the mercy of dentists,
fourteen hundred tons of job
and the chance I might drop dead
before crawling out from under it,
the possibility of reincarnation
as a business man's fat cigar,
forever puffed on, unlit in mean lips.
Like someone trying to escape through a porthole
getting their backside stuck, that's how
I felt, and that's not all, there was
a fresh bunch of flowers
tied to the bus stop down the street
again, a fresh bunch of flowers
is tied to the bus stop every Sunday.
I don't know why, I don't know
if I want to know. I don't know much
these days, but I do at least know
a terrible song when I hear one.

Small Chocolate Heart

Estimated Cycle Time:
58.8 seconds

The press opens
I open the gate
remove the mould
I spray the tool
shut the gate
I push the green button
the press closes
I trim the mould
I pack the mould

Instructions To Operator:
Remove Feedgates Flush
Check Each Shot For
Pulling And Plucking

The press opens
I open the gate
remove the mould
I spray the tool
shut the gate
I push the green button
the press closes
I trim the mould
I pack the mould

It's ten in the morning
sunny and warm outside
I'm wearing tight shoes

The press opens

I open the gate
remove the mould
I spray the tool
shut the gate
I push the green button
the press closes
I trim the mould
I pack the mould

Remember: The Next Inspection
Is By The Customer

The press opens
I open the gate
remove the mould
I spray the tool
shut the gate
I push the green button
the press closes
I trim the mould
I pack the mould

Nine hours fifty-six minutes
four point eight seconds
to go

The press opens

The Depth

Management. Two of them
and a couple of young lackeys
are in my way for half an hour
discussing the depth of the mould
coming out of the LB350
every 47.9 seconds.
'They won't wear it. I know
they won't.'
'But anything less and it would
fall off.'
I stop listening, try to carry on
as if they're not
present, as if I'm not,
as if I was under a parachute
gliding in a blue sky.
Then they are gone.
Our Quality Control Inspector
strides over.
'And what pearls of wisdom
did that lot have for you?'
They were talking, I tell him, about
the depth of the mould.
'The depth?' he says. '*The depth?*
He turns, walks back to his office
shaking his head.
'They haven't got
a clue. Haven't got
a buggerin' clue.'

It's the sort of job where you lose
something, something
you spend the weekends
looking for with tired eyes.

Powder Man

'Fuck off!' he shouts.
'Get fucked!' I shout back.
It's how Jacko and I
say hello every day,
it keeps him happy
and amuses me too.
He's the powder man
who keeps the machines going,
it's a back-breaking job.
He prowls the factory
with a head full of films
like *Full Metal Jacket*,
punching things as he goes,
people if he's that way out.
In a US Marine haircut
he'll say, 'Outta the way, Buddy.'
His neck's thicker
than some girls' waists.
'I'd shag any woman,'
he informs me,
'except for one.'
He doesn't say
which one.

No Chance

It's summer, and I stare
from where I'm stuck
trimming moulds for chocolate dog bones
across the floor at Ken,
who's fifty-seven,
who had a heart attack four years ago
during his dinner break.
There he is at the Fourteen Hundred,
hoisting hot, sharp, heavy fans,
sweat staining the back of his shirt
like a lake on a map, pouring down
his flushed forehead and face
and off the end of his nose.
He shakes his head and a thick spray
flies from his hair.
I can't watch too long, have to look away,
have to get on with my own work
which is just as tough
in this sort of heat.
I think if I had a heart attack
they wouldn't get me back in here
at gunpoint. That's obvious.
I wonder what Ken was scared of
and frown.

Summer Sick Note

We've got lavender toilet paper
made in Worksop
breakfast's on the go
I'm in the living room
watching the traffic
an endless procession
all sorts of vehicles
here on this road to Blackpool

a young black guy
in a red convertible
his shades reflecting
the bright morning sun
there goes someone with a canoe on their roof
another with a dog at the wheel
and one with a human head
stuck on the bonnet
it's going to be a hot day

my brother Dave is in Sweden
my great friend Nev, he's there as well
I'm not getting much done
but it beats the factory
beats it hands down
a bad case of the runs, I told them
it feels great to be here
with no clothes on

Bad Attitude

We each took turns
to pick a cardboard box
up off the floor,
take three self-conscious steps
in slow motion
and put it down again,
and six months later
the Works Manager
gave us fancy certificates
saying we'd attended a course
in Manual Handling.
After I'd stopped laughing
the Works Manager told me
I'd a bad attitude;
he stood gaping
like I was something odd;
'but you turn up on time,'
he added, 'and do your job,'
and then he smiled
and I smiled
and he walked back to his office.

Joy

A young Sikh with a grin drives the taxi.
'I bet there's some joy and rejoicing
going on in there this Sunday morning,'
he says as we arrive. I laugh at that
and pay him and get out, moving
slowly, clock in and go to my machine
where the night shift operator
looks just about ready to climb the wall.
He's something of a smackhead, I've been told,
and I believe it, he's certainly weird.
But who on this planet isn't,
and aren't I working seven till seven
every Saturday and Sunday
and taking taxis to the stinking place?

I've dropped on for an easy job today
but stupidly have brought nothing to read
and have to scrounge round for something. I get
The Sunday Mirror, The Sport on Sunday
and Friday's *The Sun*, and I read all three
at great length, God help me, I read all three.

Y'Know Warramean?

Everything he tells you
he follows with the phrase
Y'know warramean?
He's used to drinking every night
Y'know warramean?
I don't mean he goes out every night
he might just have a few cans in the house
Y'know warramean?
If he could get out of the habit of drinking every night
then he wouldn't have to drink every night
Y'know warramean?
And you feel like grabbing hold of him and shouting
I'M NOT THREE YEARS OLD, OF COURSE I KNOW
WHAT YOU MEAN
Y'KNOW WARRAMEAN?
But you don't do that and he carries on
Y'know warramean?

He can't do overtime at the weekends
because of his Community Service
Y'know warramean?
He got done for almost nothing
well they called it assault
Y'know warramean?
I mean you can't call it assault
all he did was shout at her in the street
Y'know warramean?
Well she told the coppers he hit her
Y'know warramean?
Well he might have pushed her slightly
Y'know warramean?
It's ok, the Community Service
it'd be ok if you were getting paid
Y'know warramean?

Boss Arse

I almost got the sack,
I almost thumped a man
for the first time in twenty years,
a short fat strutting man
who thinks he knows who he is
and who I am, but who knows
less than corrugated cardboard
cut into strips, put in a pile,
less than rusty blades in a tin.
I can hardly believe he's real.
I could hardly believe him real
even as I shook my fist in his face –
'Fuck off you fucking little cunt!'
I should have been cooler somehow,
I should have been something like a freezer;
all afternoon I behave like someone
treading round a puddle of oil,
and the odious little man
still exists, scheming
in a brightly-lit office.

Chicken Bone Charlie

The three lads in the bus station
are just about legless, shouting 'Barmy Army'
over and over
as we wait for the
Marsden Hard End. It's 7.28
on a Saturday evening. I'm on my way home
from a grim job, not exactly enhanced
by the close company of Chicken Bone Charlie,
a scruffy-arsed little ragamuffin
who got on the wrong side of me
first thing in the morning
by playing a 90-minute Meat Loaf cassette
at full volume on his ghetto blaster.
We didn't speak from 7.15 a.m. to 6 p.m.,
despite working side by side. Then I said,
'Only one hour to go,' and he replied,
'Good. I'm sick of having to look at you.'
So I said, 'Even your best friend
must be sick of looking at *you*',
then neither of us
spoke again, as the last hour
dragged its heavy feet.

The Handshake Poem

The summer's here, and the Managing Director
has just cleared out his desk, looking shaken
to be sacked for incompetence, and with rumours
of financial shenanigans and back-handers
laughed about openly on the shop-floor.

Last Christmas, he handed me a large box
of Cadbury's Milk Tray and said, glancing
at the name patch on my pale blue workshirt,
'Merry Christmas, Geoff', and shook hands with me
as though we were sealing a weapons deal.

And then, after catching me outside with a fag
when I should have been trimming lawnmower handles,
my first fag for three, nearly four long hours,
he gave me, some time in April or May,
my third written warning for misconduct.

The summer's here, and the Managing Director
has left the premises, his tail between his legs.
'They say he took ten grand from some Germans…'
We're all sure he's guilty, even if they prove him innocent.
Nothing could mar our ebullient mood.

I Did Brain Surgery On A Barnsley Pub Floor

Wayne by the juke-box
lost an eye at the weekend,
Wayne watching Wayne
and Wayne playing pool
broke both his arms –
he was complaining
he couldn't wipe his backside.

Wayne walked in
with a dog's skull in the palm of his hand –
'Alas, poor Wayne,
my fair sister,' he said.
He sat down at the bar,
in between Wayne
and Wayne.

Wayne proposed a toast
to Wayne,
but Wayne, Wayne and Wayne
refused to drink
and left in a bit of a huff.
'John Wayne films!
I bloody well can't stand them!'

shouted Wayne,
the uninjured one with the moustache.
I took my scalpel out,
introduced myself –
'Hello, I'm a surgeon
of some renown,
Dr. Wayne...'

His Fingernails

I told him his hands were someone else's,
it was their fingernails he'd been chewing,
but he just laughed, as if I was joking.

So I pulled out a large brown envelope,
photographic evidence and so on,
dropped it on the table in front of him.

He stared at it and then he picked it up.
I tapped my feet and hummed 'Smokestack Lightning'
as he tried to take it all in, and then

he was sobbing and my arm was round him.
There, there, I said, you'll feel better later.
I was lying. He'd never feel better.

He Dreamed He Burst Balloons

He dreamed he burst balloons for a living
and was his own supervisor.
He worked twelve hours a week, made a good wage.

He was never exhausted, never bored.
He was calm like a cat full of tuna,
calm like a yacht in a sunlit harbour.

His past life had been forgotten
like a dull episode of a cop show.
There were no scars on his body.

Sleepless

He woke just after one a.m.
to the familiar sound
of a police helicopter
circling over the mill, down the canal.
Naked in the darkness, he stood and watched.
Something seemed to be taking place
beneath the thick, dark trees.

The bastards had ruined his sleep.
He rolled a spliff, just a single-skinner,
some homegrown stuff, smoked it on the sofa
as the coppers hovered,
probing with their stupid spotlight
for any sign of life.

Red Dungarees
for TVR and Nichola

'Thank God,' she said, 'Friday, some music please,'
and she placed her bare feet on top of mine
beneath the table. She was somewhat hoarse

from shouting all day long, but a few drinks
soon put that right. I put 'Abbey Road' on,
it sounded great. George Harrison had died

the day before. 'I think I may have to
buy some new clothes,' I said, 'and stop smoking.'
They were two things I'd never said before

and her eyebrows went up. I lit a smoke.
'Know any shops that sell red dungarees?'
We sat there drunk and ha-ed and ho-ed and hee-ed.

P For Poem

I'm tired, slumped in a chair,
struggling to take it in –

aircraft crashing,
buildings collapsing,

dust and smoke and holy shit
everywhere.

Things can only get worse,
I mean better.

I can hear Death's Boots
shuffling on the Welcome mat –

'I don't need anything right now!'
I shout.

Sofa Factory

I was following a series
of red-lettered signposts:
SOFA FACTORY,
and an arrow, pointing.
I was wondering
if it said SOFA FACTORY
on every street-corner in town.
Then I came to a yard
with some huge iron gates
and above the gates in red paint:
SOFA FACTORY.

The job was dead easy.
All I had to do
was stick sofa catalogues
into envelopes,
put an address label on the front
and stamp them
second-class postage paid.
I kept looking at the clock.
I kept looking at it
like I couldn't believe it.

There were four of us
at a large table.
The others were young blacks.
One of them asked me
if I was an alky.
He said I had that look
about me.
The other two laughed
and I smiled and said
I couldn't afford to be an alky.
Which seemed to be an answer
everyone could live with.

Sixteen At A Time

I'm getting paid
minimum wage
to pack screws in plastic bags
sixteen at a time.
I'm working with a teenage girl
who's just had a ring
put in her eyebrow,
plays with it all the time.
She's what you'd call a chatterbox,
and always seems to be lurching
from one domestic crisis
to another. I get to hear
about her boyfriend, who has a steel plate
in his skull and sometimes
smashes the furniture – who once tried
to throw himself through
Burton's Menswear front window
but just bounced off,
went to sleep on the pavement.

Becky's ok, I like her. I told her
I was tired of having to listen
to Pulse radio, I wanted
Howlin' Wolf, Muddy Waters, Captain Beefheart –
'Whoever they're supposed to be!'
she said, laughing.
'People you've never heard of
might turn out to be the best people,'
I said. She said,
'How interesting.'
Then she asked if I wanted
a piece of her Yorkie
and I replied no thanks.

Pretty Funny Things

It's hot in this hell-hole,
bastard roasting.
Half the women
sit in open blouses,
cleavage and patterned bras
and navel jewellery
all showing.

I've overheard some
pretty funny things,
like two eighteen-year-old girls
discussing cocksucking.
They had this conversation
in front of me in the canteen,
while I chewed my
cheese sandwiches and they
slurped chicken pot noodles.
To spit or to swallow,
that was the question.

Then there's Ugly Darren,
who brags about wanking
with his dirty socks round his cock.
One girl asked him
how many women he'd had sex with.
'Let me think… can you count
your sisters and your mam?'

The Next Break

Working for this
tinpot agency.
They like me too
tired to think straight.
I spent eight hours today
folding paper in half
and sealing envelopes
in a large, cold room
with some other losers.
More than two hundred people
in rows of ten,
all of them
blathering
on and on,
or singing along
to the loud radios,
all the radios tuned
to the same crap station.
The sort of job
where all the time
you live only
for the next break,
the next chance
to stand outside smoking
in the freezing wind and rain.

Stand-In

I'm standing-in
for a suicidal man,
doing his job.
It's boring, boring
like the life of a nail
in an old box.
I stand with folded arms
and yawn and watch
a circular saw
relentlessly spin,
stamping my boots
to keep my eyes open.

I wonder about him,
this man I've never met.
Everything I use
has his name on
in black felt pen
in capitals: LAWRENCE.
I know he's fifty-one,
off work with depression.
I know no one else here
likes him that much.
No one talks about him.
Asking gets me nowhere:
'Lawrence is Lawrence.'
That's all they'll give me.

Stupid Stuff

The supervisor
had something on his mind:
'Every time
you open a paper
there's some celebrity
showing their arse,
what's wrong
with these people?'
I thought about this
and other stupid stuff
as I toted heavy cardboard boxes
full of personnel files
up three flights of stairs.
Fifty-seven trips
on one of the hottest
days of the year.
Tom said he'd report me
to the union
for sweating on the job.
But we don't have a union.
Then we heard on the radio
that Dennis Thatcher
had passed on.
Shirley said, 'Poor Maggie',
and I laughed.
But to her it was no joke.
Funny how you can
go off people.
Well, I'm sure she's gone off
me too.

Small Man in a Small Town

The supervisor
had something on his mind:
'The world would be
a better place
if we killed ten pakis
every morning.'
My God, you have to put up
with some shit
if you want to keep a job
nowadays.
Fifteen minutes later
he's back, telling me
asylum seekers
should be castrated
so they can't fuck
any English women.
I'm not kidding,
I have to listen to this
every day
from seven thirty till five,
when I make my dash for
freedom.
I stand at the bus stop
smoking
as stones clatter
the roof of the shelter
thrown by kids
from a bridge
over the road.
Nice kids
with nice dads
with love
in their hearts.

That Was Your Life

I can't believe how fast
it all goes by,

seven years from now I'll be sitting round
and I'll be fifty-three.

Sixteen years from now I'll be sitting round
and I'll be sixty-two.

Twenty years ago I was sitting round
and I was twenty-six.

All Weekend

He tried to ignore it.
He took all his clothes off,
slumped down at the kitchen table.
He smoked a lot, coughing a lot.

He paced about the room.
He stood at the window, stared out.
'I can't stand it!' he said aloud,
but he knew he'd have to.

Under Strict Orders

She banned him from the living room
at her thirteenth birthday party.
She was sure he'd embarrass her
in front of all her friends.
She told him straight: she was growing up.
He was no longer required
to play the fool, blow balloons up
or supervise pass the parcel.
He was a prehistoric fart
best left alone in the kitchen
with his bottles of wine
and personal stereo.

He was whistling
'Mr Tambourine Man'
when she burst in
and told him to shut up.
He came *that close*
to embarrassing her.

Chicken Cashew Nuts

There's a full moon tonight
over Salendine Nook
as he looks out licking his lips.
They took more than two hours
to deliver the meal
three quarters of a mile.
His fortune cookie says
there is a lot of stuff
he wants out of his life,
stuff like desks, swivel chairs
and prats sitting in them.

Suddenly he comes round
in a roomful of aliens
from the planet Solemn.
Luckily he's wearing
his brand new silver-grey
attitude coat.

Man Enduring Heatwave

He's sitting there
wearing nothing
but underpants.

He's only wearing those
because
he's no curtains.

*

He's come up with a list –
ten things he needs to start doing.
That's a load off his mind.

He feels like getting drunk, celebrating.
In fact he already did, yesterday.
But he feels like celebrating again.

*

He's way deep into
John Coltrane's
A Love Supreme –

finds it hard to believe
Coltrane's favourite dish
was fried brains.

Unshaven Poem

God save us from the professors.
They're a hard to please bunch alright.
All they need do is open the packet
and they're the world's biggest experts.
There's a kind of night

when all I'm good for
is connecting with the world wide cobweb
to take on other fools at backgammon.
It's a sad way to go, I need slapping.
I'll be growing a beard if I'm not careful.

Stockings and Slippers

Jeanette's hanging
stockings
out on the line.

I watch
from the kitchen
with her sister.

She won't wear them
herself, she says,
stockings,

she just can't get
on with
suspender belts.

I say I need
a new pair of
slippers;

it's no joke,
I need them,
I'm serious.

Then Jeanette's back:
'That's that
bloody job done.'

Working Through

Once they got going
the band weren't too bad
for a bunch of old drunks,
I was there till
after midnight.
I hardly slept at all
and the next day
on the machine
was living hell.
It was one of
the hottest days
of the year
and one of
the hardest jobs
I'd had.
I started out
at seven a.m.
thinking
I'd never
make it.
But like a nail
working through
an old shoe
it slowly
turned into
seven
p.m.
and I was still
breathing
and I still knew
who I was.

When You're Pushing Fifty

When you're pushing fifty
it gets harder to wake
to shake off the drink
shave with a clear head
get out in time for the bus
do a hard day's labour
the sweat pouring out of you
with a bitter smell

When you're pushing fifty
you've dreamt most of your dreams
can't recall them now
all that remains
are the motions you go through
saying the same things
as if you still meant them
through what's left of your teeth

When you're pushing fifty
you've read all the great books
know there are none to come
you don't believe in miracles
you no longer hope
for social change
know phonies and killers
will always be in charge

When you're pushing fifty
you've suffered a lot of fools
now you show them the door
you just follow your own nose
it's smelled most stuff by now
it knows bullshit for instance

it can smell a rat
or a rare flower

When you're pushing fifty
you know you don't know everything
you know enough
you know just as much as you can take
you know a good move when you see it
or a bad mistake
there's a lid on your rage
now and then you hear it hissing

Scotching The Seagull Rumour

It was a gaggle of geese
that chased us off the beach,
who'd be scared of seagulls?
Twenty-five geese though
all running at you
wings outstretched,
that's an amazing sight.
And the noise they made!

Later we took a cruise
on a paddle steamer
down the River Clyde,
saw dolphins alongside
leaping out of the water
just like in the movies.

Moose Face, Wobble and Plonk

Michael Bruce got voted Chest Of The Year
by the readers of *Smash Hits* in '71,
but Yvonne Plonk revealed she fancied me
because I resembled one of The Sweet,
especially my mouth shared the shape of his.
This information made me feel quite sick –
only now can I speak of it lightly,
three hundred thousand cigarettes later.

The other girls who courted me back then
were Moose Face and Wobble, neither of whom
made me feel like dancing. Their name for me
was Mad Geoff. They had this running joke –
if you're going to have one sore tit
you might as well have two. It was over my head,
as were so many things. I was posing like mad
and this took up most of my energy.

Looking Hard, Feeling Mean

Ben shouted down to come on up.
I was in the middle of the living room floor,
playing air guitar to 'School's Out'.
A pall of smoke hung in the air,
empty cans of Skol were scattered around.
The song finished, 'Looney Tune' started up,
I walked to the foot of the stairs,
up the stairs. There was no light at all,
four closed doors. Where are you? I shouted.
A bedroom door opened and there they were,
Ben and Roy, no clothes on, full erections.
Roy's cock was huge, Ben's puny next to it.
Ben got hold of Roy's cock, yanking it up and down.
They were both laughing, I stood there watching
then I turned round, went back downstairs,
sat on the sofa, lit a cigarette,
found a can of Skol with a bit still in,
listened to the rest of Side One, stood up
and took the record off, put it back in its sleeve,
the famous sleeve in the shape of a desk
with a pair of knickers inside.
I held the album in my right hand
and left the house, walked home
through streets full of sunlight, full of
women and pushchairs and babies, old men,
walked home realising my best two friends
weren't people I thought I ever wanted
to set eyes on again.

Don't Lean On The Sideboard

I was always accused by Grace
of stopping her clock
by leaning on the sideboard –
'Don't lean on the sideboard
you'll stop the clock!'
became a catchphrase among my cronies,
something someone would come out with
at a boring football match or
brooding as we walked home
from the school dance.

The very first time I got drunk,
I mean so drunk I couldn't stand,
I said it to the doctor who examined me
in the Emergency Department
of Barnsley General Hospital –
'Don't lean on the sideboard
you'll stop the clock!'
I slurred, laughing
like it was the funniest thing
anybody had ever said.

Sunrise

Sunrise –
a fat man
running from his bed
wearing only a vest
is a much less
beautiful sight,
as is a cat
eating a moth,
as is an ashtray
full of death.
Things can get funny
when you've had no sleep
as if they weren't
funny already.
A long way off
maybe a dog will bark,
my chest will wheeze
like a faulty machine
and a number of wasps
will be trying to get
in here.

Nobody said
they wanted this
war all the time,
they weren't asked.
The world's full of
empty stomachs,
they'll have to stay like that.
Family viewing's
making a comeback.